12 TIPS FOR A
HEALTHY DIET

by Marne Ventura

STORY
LIBRARY

www.12StoryLibrary.com

12-Story Library is an imprint of Peterson Publishing Company and Press Room Editions.

Produced for 12-Story Library by Red Line Editorial

Photographs ©: EpicStockMedia/Shutterstock Images, cover, 1; leonori/Shutterstock Images, 4; TL Studio/Shutterstock Images, 5; Ana Blazic Pavlovic/Shutterstock Images, 6, 29; ducu59us/Shutterstock Images, 7; Scorpp/Shutterstock Images, 8; mama mia/Shutterstock Images, 9; Brent Hofacker/Shutterstock Images, 10, 21, 28; Jacek Chabraszewski/Shutterstock Images, 11; Tatiana Volgutova/Shutterstock Images, 12; Golden Pixels LLC/Shutterstock Images, 13; Matthew Bechelli/Shutterstock Images, 14; davidsansegundo/Shutterstock Images, 15; Julie Clopper/Shutterstock Images, 16; Samuel Borges Photography/Shutterstock Images, 17; Stephen Coburn/Shutterstock Images, 18; Niloo/Shutterstock Images, 19; Gossip/Shutterstock Images, 20; Ildi Papp/Shutterstock Images, 22; Lilyana Vynogradova/Shutterstock Images, 23; Ekaterina Minaeva/Shutterstock Images, 24; dlewis33/iStockphoto, 25; SolStock/iStockphoto, 26; stockcreations/Shutterstock Images, 27

Library of Congress Cataloging-in-Publication Data
Cataloging-in-publication information is on file with the Library of Congress.
978-1-63235-365-8 (hardcover)
978-1-63235-383-2 (paperback)
978-1-62143-507-5 (hosted ebook)

Printed in the United States of America
Mankato, MN
May, 2016

Access free, up-to-date content on this topic plus a full digital version of this book. Scan the QR code on page 31 or use your school's login at 12StoryLibrary.com.

Table of Contents

Choose Fruit Often

Have you heard the saying "an apple a day keeps the doctor away"? Apples, like all fruits, contain vitamins. These are nutrients your cells need to work well and keep you healthy. Vitamins help your eyes see better in dim light. They also help you see different colors. Vitamins help you make red blood cells, and they turn food into energy. They help your skin heal when you get a cut. They help your bones grow strong.

You also need minerals for health. Fruits are a good source of minerals. Some help your brain, spinal cord, and nerves work together to control your body. Others keep your muscles working. Some help red blood cells carry oxygen through your body. Others keep your bones healthy.

The vitamins in fruit make your immune system stronger so you can fight off sickness.

Like vitamins, minerals help your body fight off infection and heal after a cut.

Fruit is loaded with fiber. Fiber is the part of a plant that your body can't digest. It makes you feel full before you overeat. Fiber passes through your body and carries away waste. It causes sugar to be moved into your blood more slowly, so you have a steady stream of energy.

In addition to being so good for you, fruit makes a perfect snack or dessert because it tastes sweet.

46.5
Average pounds (21.1 kg) of fresh fruit eaten every year by each American.

- Fruits give you important vitamins and minerals.
- Fiber in fruits has many benefits.
- Fruits are naturally sweet.
- Fruits make a healthy snack or dessert.

Another bonus is that many fruits are ready to eat and travel well. Oranges, tangerines, and bananas even have their own wrappers!

Grapes or plums need only a quick rinsing.

Find Your Favorite Vegetables

Nutrition experts put vegetables into five groups. The first group is dark green vegetables. This includes spinach and broccoli. Starchy vegetables are the second group. This includes potatoes and corn. The third group is red and orange vegetables. Tomatoes and carrots are in this group. Beans and peas are the fourth group. The fifth group is for all other vegetables. This group includes lettuce, onions, and many more choices.

Vegetables are nutrient dense. They contain a lot of vitamins, minerals, and fiber. And they do not have many calories. This makes them a smart choice for meals and snacks.

Eat vegetables with other foods you like. Enjoy cucumber slices with low-fat dip. Add sunflower seeds to a lettuce salad. Sweet potatoes and chili peppers taste great in soups. Add zucchini to homemade muffins. Toss peas into macaroni and cheese.

Taste different vegetables until you find a favorite from each group.

Frozen vegetables are a convenient way to get the health benefits of fresh vegetables.

Fresh vegetables are delicious and nutritious. Frozen vegetables are also a good choice. After vegetables are picked, they begin to lose nutrients. Frozen vegetables are preserved right away. That means their nutrients remain until you're ready to eat them.

100
Percent of vegetables that contain vitamin C.

- Eat vegetables from all five groups.
- Vegetables are nutrient dense.
- Combine raw and cooked vegetables with other foods you like.
- Frozen vegetables are a good alternative to fresh.

EAT BRIGHT COLORS

Plant foods contain phytochemicals. These chemicals are what give plants their color. One type is found in red and dark pink foods. Another is found in orange and dark green leafy foods. Recent studies show that phytochemicals have health benefits. Eat a variety of colorful vegetables to get different phytochemicals.

Go for Whole Grains

When choosing bread or cereals, whole grains are best for you. Whole grains contain all of the original seed parts. Sometimes millers remove some or all of the parts of the grain. They do this by cracking, crushing, cooking, or rolling the grains.

Grain seeds are made up of three parts. The first part is the endosperm. It's the starchy part of the seed. The second part is the bran. That's the outer husk. It's a rich source of fiber. The third part is the germ. This part nourishes the seed. It's a great source of vitamins and minerals.

Whole-grain bread is much healthier than white bread.

Plain popcorn is a healthy snack made from whole grains.

Millers make white flour by grinding whole wheat and removing the bran and germ. When they do this, nutrients are lost. Whole grain flour is a healthier choice. That's because it contains the bran and germ.

Grains are a good source of carbohydrates. These are your body's main source of energy. Whole grains are complex carbohydrates. It takes your body longer to digest them than foods without fiber. As a result, you get a longer, slower stream of energy.

Look for ways to add whole grains to your meals. For breakfast, enjoy oatmeal with low-fat milk and fruit. Make sandwiches for lunch with 100 percent whole wheat bread. Try quinoa for dinner.

THINK ABOUT IT

Why do you think millers sometimes remove parts of the grain? How might this affect the grain's flavor?

3

Minimum number of daily servings of whole grains recommended for children aged 9–13.

- A whole grain is a seed kernel from a cereal plant.
- Whole grains include the endosperm, bran, and germ.
- Whole grains provide vitamins, minerals, and fiber.
- Whole grains provide energy in the form of carbohydrates.

Choose Healthy Fats

Foods from plants and animals contain fats. Your body needs fat to work well. But there are different kinds of fats. Some are better for you than others.

Unsaturated fats are one kind of fat. They are in plant foods such as avocados, nuts, and seeds. They are also in fish such as salmon and tuna. The fats in these foods are good for your heart. They also help your body keep a steady supply of energy so you feel well.

Unsaturated fats are good for your blood vessels and kidneys. Choose these fats most often.

THINK ABOUT IT

Processed foods are inexpensive products that have a long shelf life. Margarine is a processed food that contains unhealthy trans fats. Can you think of any processed foods that help people stay healthy?

Eating tuna is a tasty way to get the healthy fats your body needs.

Meat contains many nutrients, but it also contains unhealthy saturated fats.

Saturated fats are another kind of fat. They are in foods that come from animals. These include meat, butter, and milk. It's okay to eat these foods, because they have other nutrients. However, too much saturated fat is not healthy.

Trans fats are a third kind of fat. They are in some margarine, baked goods, and fried foods. Learn to read food labels. Try to stay away from foods that contain trans fats. They are harmful to your heart health.

19
Maximum percent of saturated fat that cooking oils or fats should contain.

- Your body needs healthy fats.
- Choose fats from plants and fish most often.
- Saturated fats come from animals.
- Try to avoid trans fats.

MACRONUTRIENTS AND MICRONUTRIENTS

Food gives you nutrition in two forms. Macronutrients are one form. They include carbohydrates, protein, and fats. Your body needs large amounts of macronutrients. Micronutrients are the other form. They include vitamins, minerals, and water. Your body needs smaller amounts of micronutrients.

5

Find the Right Balance of Diet and Exercise

You need energy from food to live. This energy is measured in units called calories. Each gram of protein or carbohydrate supplies four calories. Each gram of fat supplies nine calories. The more vitamins, minerals, and fiber a food supplies per calorie, the more nutrient dense it is. Foods that give you calories without nutrition are sources of empty calories.

The more energy you use, the more calories you need. People who sit for most of the day don't need as much food as people who are active. As a general rule, if people eat more than they need, they gain weight. The reverse is also true. An active person who doesn't eat enough food will burn body fat and lose weight.

Potatoes are a delicious example of a nutrient-dense food.

60
Minutes per day kids and teens should spend being active.

- Energy from food is measured in calories.
- Eating more calories than you burn results in stored fat.
- Using more calories than you eat results in burned fat.
- Aim to eat mostly nutrient-dense calories.

ACTIVITY IS AWESOME

Moving a lot every day has many benefits. Health experts say children who get plenty of exercise are likely to feel good about themselves. They also do better in school, keep healthier body weights, and have stronger bones and muscles. They sleep better, too!

To stay at a healthy weight, it's important to balance the amount of food you eat with the amount of exercise you do. Being active every day helps you maintain a healthy weight. It also keeps your heart healthy. Choose wholesome foods. Avoid empty calories. Enjoy soccer, hiking, biking, swimming, and dancing. You'll have fun, feel good, and help your body stay strong.

Hiking is a healthy activity that lets you enjoy nature.

6

Drink Low-Fat Milk or Water

Drinking enough water every day is vital to good health. Water keeps your body at the right temperature. It helps your joints work well. It protects your spinal cord and other tissues. Taking in plenty of water helps your body get rid of waste.

Milk is also a good drink for meals and snacks. It provides calcium and vitamin D. These nutrients help build strong bones and healthy teeth. Unsweetened, low-fat, and nonfat milk are the best choices.

Sodas, energy drinks, sports drinks, and fruit drinks are not smart choices for everyday drinks. They are high in sugar and often have no other nutrients. They can cause

A slice of lemon or lime can make plain water taste more interesting.

weight gain and tooth decay. Fruit juice is better than sweetened fruit drinks because it has vitamins and minerals. But a piece of whole fruit is a better choice than juice because it's packed with fiber. If you have orange juice with breakfast, choose milk or water for the rest of the day. If you like sweetened drinks, save them for special occasions.

How much water is enough? It's different for everyone. If the weather is warm or you've been active, you might need extra water. Pay attention to your thirst, and be prepared. Carry a bottle of water with you when you leave home. Try sparkling water with a squeeze of orange juice for a change.

60
Percent of body weight that is water.

- Water helps your body function properly.
- Plain water is a healthy choice.
- Low-fat milk provides calcium and vitamin D.
- Sweetened drinks are empty calories.

Fruit juice contains lots of nutrients, but it is not as good for you as whole fruit.

Save Sugar for Special Occasions

Fruits and dairy products contain natural sugars. They taste sweet without added sugar. But many other foods have sugar added to them. Foods containing natural sugar are better for your health than foods with added sugar.

Sugar gives you energy. Energy from fruit and dairy products comes with added nutrients. These nutrients include fiber, vitamins, and minerals. On the other hand, foods with added sugar, such as candy or cookies, do not have these nutrients. These sugars are empty calories. So, choose your calories wisely!

Foods with added sugar, such as candy, can cause tooth decay.

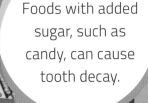

NAMES FOR ADDED SUGAR

When reading food labels, try to choose foods without added sugars. There are many kinds. They include white sugar, brown sugar, molasses, high fructose corn syrup, and honey. Other names for added sugar are fructose, dextrose, sucrose, fruit juice concentrate, corn syrup, and maple syrup.

Eating too much added sugar can cause unhealthy weight gain. If you fill up on empty calories, you might not be hungry for food with important nutrients. And too much added sugar can make your blood sugar levels high. If this happens often over a long period of time, it can cause other health problems.

11

Teaspoons of added sugar in a 12-ounce (355 mL) soda.

- Fruits and dairy products contain natural sugar plus nutrients.
- Added sugars do not contain nutrients.
- Too much sugar can lead to health problems.
- Save sugary treats for special occasions.

Some examples are damage to your heart, blood vessels, and kidneys.

A sugary treat is fine once in a while, but choosing natural sugars for everyday foods will keep you healthy.

Enjoy Whole, Natural Foods

A whole food is a plant or animal food that is in its natural state. It hasn't been processed or refined. It doesn't have artificial ingredients added to it. Choose whole foods over refined, processed foods whenever you can.

Like grains, fruits and vegetables are best eaten whole. For example, most of the fiber and vitamins in an apple are in the skin. So, applesauce has fewer nutrients than a whole apple. That's because the skin has been removed.

Health experts recommend shopping along the perimeter of a grocery store because that's where most of the whole foods are.

Food producers look for ways to make food taste better and last longer. Sometimes this leads to packaged foods that are not as nutritious as natural foods. Added sugars and refined grains are found in many ready-to-eat foods. High amounts of salt and unhealthy fats are common. Food makers use artificial flavors and colors to make their products more appealing. Sometimes chemicals are used to make food last longer.

Packaged foods often contain extra ingredients that make them less healthy.

For better health, eat whole, simple foods more often than refined, processed foods. You'll get more nutrients and fewer empty calories.

45
Percent of recommended daily vitamin C in a baked potato.

- Whole foods are foods in their natural state.
- Healthful parts of foods are often missing in refined foods.
- Processed foods can contain added sugar, artificial ingredients, unhealthy fats, and too much sodium.
- Whole foods are more nutritious than processed foods.

SODIUM

Sodium is a mineral that your heart and blood need to work properly. You get sodium from salt. Too much sodium can be harmful to your heart and blood. Canned vegetables can be high in sodium, so rinse them well. Make your own sauces and baked goods to avoid high-sodium ingredients.

Eat throughout the Day

When you eat, your body digests food. The food is broken down into smaller parts. Carbohydrates in food are turned to sugar and sent into your bloodstream. Your cells absorb this sugar and use it for energy. As the cells take the sugar from the blood, stored sugar is released from your liver into your bloodstream. This is your body's way of making sure all of its parts have the energy they need to work properly.

When you eat enough healthy foods, your body has the fuel it needs to work well. If you go too long without eating, your blood sugar drops. You might feel tired or unwell. You might not have the energy to do your best at school or while playing sports. If you let yourself get too hungry

Nuts make a great snack between meals.

A healthy breakfast gives you the energy you need to get your day started.

between meals, you might overeat at the next meal. Also, you are more likely to make unhealthy choices.

Eat breakfast, lunch, and dinner every day. Balance your meals by filling half of your plate with fruits and vegetables. Fill one-fourth of your plate with lean protein. And fill one-fourth with a starchy food. Add a bit of healthy fat, and drink water or milk. If you're hungry between meals, have a small snack. The best choices are fruits and vegetables. Lean protein, healthy fat, and whole grains are also good.

2,000
Number of calories the average 9- to 13-year-old needs each day.

- Eat three meals a day and one or two snacks.
- Carbohydrates from food give the body energy in the form of sugar.
- Low blood sugar can make you feel tired or unwell.
- Eat every three to four hours.

21

Pick Lean Protein

Much of your body is made of protein. That includes your hair, skin, muscles, and bones. When you eat foods that contain protein, your body breaks it into smaller proteins that do different jobs. Some help the red blood cells carry oxygen to all the parts of your body. Others are used to build and repair muscles.

Proteins are like long chains. Each link of the chain is an amino acid. Different proteins contain different amino acids. There are 22 amino acids that you need to stay healthy. Your body makes 13 of them. You need to get the other nine from foods. These are called essential amino acids.

Some foods contain all nine essential amino acids. They include meat, poultry, eggs, dairy, fish, quinoa, and soybeans. Many other protein-rich foods contain less than nine. They include beans, nuts, and

Quinoa is a high-protein seed that tastes great when mixed into salads.

many vegetables. When you eat a variety of healthy foods, the amino acids combine to form protein chains in your body. It's not difficult to get enough protein. If you eat enough calories from a wide variety of healthy foods, you will get plenty of protein.

Protein-rich plants are a smart choice. In addition to protein, they give you fiber, vitamins, and minerals. Nuts, seeds, and legumes contain healthy fat.

Animal proteins supply lots of nutrients. The best choices are fish, skinless poultry, eggs, and low-fat

15
Percent of calories from protein in the average American diet.

- Much of your body is made of protein.
- Protein from food helps your body grow and repair itself.
- Amino acids combine to form protein chains.
- Eating a variety of wholesome foods gives you enough protein.

dairy. Fatty meats and whole dairy products are high in saturated fat, so try to limit these.

Beans are low in fat and high in protein.

Read the Food Label

Most of the foods you buy have nutrition facts printed on the package. This label gives you information to make smart food choices. Look for and read food labels. Compare different foods, and decide which are healthiest.

First look for the ingredients list. This tells you what the food is made of. Ingredients are listed in order from most to least. If the first ingredient on a box of cereal is sugar, there is more sugar in the cereal than any other ingredient. Whole-grain, rolled oats are the only ingredient in a box of plain oatmeal. Look for foods with wholesome ingredients that you recognize. Avoid

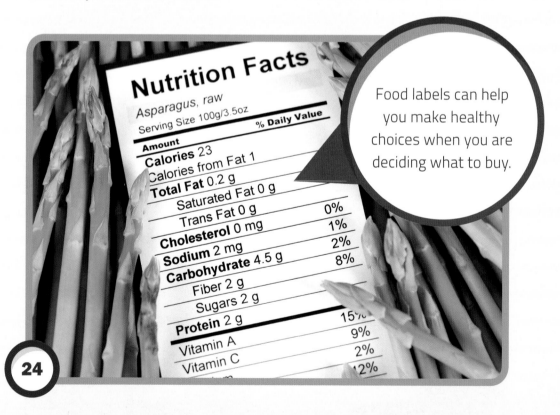

Nutrition Facts

Asparagus, raw
Serving Size 100g/3.5oz

	% Daily Value
Amount	
Calories 23	
Calories from Fat 1	
Total Fat 0.2 g	
Saturated Fat 0 g	
Trans Fat 0 g	0%
Cholesterol 0 mg	1%
Sodium 2 mg	2%
Carbohydrate 4.5 g	8%
Fiber 2 g	
Sugars 2 g	
Protein 2 g	15%
Vitamin A	9%
Vitamin C	2%
	12%

Food labels can help you make healthy choices when you are deciding what to buy.

Many packaged foods are high in sodium, sugar, and saturated fat.

foods with long lists that contain high fructose corn syrup, artificial flavors, hydrogenated fats, and chemicals.

Next look at the nutrition facts on the food label. You will find the serving size and number of calories per serving. You'll also find total fat, saturated fat, trans fat, and unsaturated fat. You'll find the facts for other nutrients, including carbohydrates, protein, vitamins, and minerals.

Use the food label to help you choose foods that give you the most nutrients for the fewest calories. If there are unhealthy fats, added sugars, and too much sodium,

choose a healthier food. Look for foods that are highest in fiber, vitamins, and minerals.

100
Number of calories per serving in a moderate-calorie food.

- Most foods are labeled with nutrition facts.
- Ingredients are listed from most to least.
- Foods with short ingredients lists and wholesome ingredients are best.
- Nutrition facts help you compare foods and make wise choices.

Have Fun in the Garden, Market, and Kitchen

One of the best ways to enjoy healthy food is to help grow, buy, and prepare it. You'll have fun and get some exercise, too. You might even discover a new food that you love.

Does your family have a vegetable garden or fruit tree? If so, you can help with the planting, weeding, and picking. If you don't have a garden, you can plant parsley or basil seeds in a pot. Set the pot near a window that gets light every day. Watch your seeds sprout and grow. Once your herbs are grown, snip what you need.

When you help with the cooking, you're more likely to get meals you enjoy.

Ask if you can come along to the grocery store. Use what you've learned about healthy eating to make good food choices. Try new fruits and vegetables. Read food labels to compare foods.

Offer to help make meals at home. You can wash and cut up lettuce and your favorite vegetables for a salad. Learn to make your own baked goods instead of buying them. Use half whole grain flour in place of white flour in muffins or cookies. Use less sugar, and add naturally sweet ingredients, such as raisins or chopped apples. Use liquid vegetable oil instead of butter, and add chopped nuts for protein.

$2.24
Average cost per person for a meal at home.

- Grow your own food in a garden or pot.
- Help with shopping to practice making healthy choices.
- Help with cooking so you'll have food choices you like.
- Learn to make meals and snacks using wholesome foods.

By helping out in the kitchen, you'll have what you like to eat. You'll learn new skills that you can use as you get older. And it's fun to share what you've made with your family and friends!

You can add herbs to soup or pasta sauce.

Fact Sheet

- The stronger the bones you build while you're young, the stronger your skeleton will be for the rest of your life. Include low-fat milk, yogurt, or cheese every day. If you can't drink milk, eat other sources of calcium like dark green vegetables, beans, and almonds. Do weight-bearing activities such as running, gymnastics, and skating.

- Magazines, diet books, and television shows claim that certain "super foods" will make you healthy, thin, and free from disease. There is no single food that guarantees health. Eating a wide variety of fruits, vegetables, whole grains, healthy protein, and low-fat dairy is the smart way to eat.

- Activity is the perfect sidekick to a healthy diet. Use all the different parts of your body throughout each week. Walk, run, swim, and ride a bike. Get together with friends and play sports or go for a hike. Turn on some music and dance.

- Check your local library for healthy cookbooks. Look online for recipes to try. Good resources are available on television, too. Make your own bread with whole grains. Combine your favorite vegetables in a pot of soup. Pizza is healthy when it's made with whole grains and low-fat cheese.

- Cut back on added sugars by making your own desserts. Top a cake with fresh, sliced strawberries and a dab of whipped cream instead of frosting. Combine kiwi, sliced banana, and pineapple with yogurt and a little honey. Puree frozen bananas with vanilla extract.

Glossary

calorie
The unit used to measure the energy in food.

digest
To break down food for use by the body.

energy
The power to be active.

fiber
The indigestible material in plant foods.

macronutrients
Fats, carbohydrates, and proteins in foods.

micronutrients
Vitamins and minerals in foods.

minerals
Nonliving elements found in nature.

nutrients
The substances in food that promote health.

nutrition
The process of taking in and using food.

oxygen
An element found in nature that is needed for life.

phytochemicals
Compounds found in plants.

tissue
A group of cells that work together in the body.

vitamins
Tiny substances in foods that are needed for health.

For More Information

Books

Hunt, Sara. *Stay Fit: Your Guide to Staying Active.* Mankato, MN: Capstone, 2012.

Schrier, Allyson Valentine. *Eat Right: Your Guide to Maintaining a Healthy Diet.* Mankato, MN: Capstone, 2012.

Ventura, Marne. *The 12 Biggest Breakthroughs in Food Technology.* North Mankato, MN: 12-Story Library, 2015.

Visit 12StoryLibrary.com

Scan the code or use your school's login at **12StoryLibrary.com** for recent updates about this topic and a full digital version of this book. Enjoy free access to:

- Digital ebook
- Breaking news updates
- Live content feeds
- Videos, interactive maps, and graphics
- Additional web resources

Note to educators: Visit 12StoryLibrary.com/register to sign up for free premium website access. Enjoy live content plus a full digital version of every 12-Story Library book you own for every student at your school.

Index

About the Author

Marne Ventura is the author of more than 30 children's books. A former elementary school teacher, she holds a master's degree in education from the University of California.